THE INVISIBLE SUN

THE INVISIBLE SUN

A GUIDE FOR THE SOUL FROM RUMI'S MASTER

ATTAR

COLLECTED, EDITED, AND TRANSLATED
BY SHOLEH WOLPÉ

HARPERPERENNIAL
An Imprint of HarperCollins *Publishers*

First published in India by Harper Perennial 2025
An imprint of HarperCollins *Publishers*
HarperCollins *Publishers* India, Cyber City,
Building 10-A, Gurugram, Haryana – 122002, India
www.harpercollins.co.in

2 4 6 8 10 9 7 5 3 1

P-ISBN: 978-93-6989-776-6
E-ISBN: 978-93-6989-568-7

Designed by Yvonne Chan

Printed and bound at
Replika Press Pvt. Ltd.

MIX
Paper | Supporting responsible forestry
FSC™ C016779

This book is produced from independently certified FSC® paper to ensure responsible forest management.

HarperCollins *Publishers*, Macken House, 39/40 Mayor Street Upper, Dublin 1, D01 C9W8, Ireland

For Skyler, Ivy, and Elizabeth

These verses are magic:
more potent with each reading.

Contents

Introduction

The central idea in Sufism is that the soul, in the prison of the body, awaits release. Once freed, it returns to the Source, the Creator. However, you can experience this reunion while still bound in your physical form by looking inward and by purification. Sufis believe that the path to this union is not found through studying religious texts, but rather through approaching that Unknowable Being through love.

The mind can't master the art of love.
Love cannot engage in the brain.

Open your heart's eyes
and fuse with the universe.

If you open only the mind's eyes,
you will never see love in full.

If denial and damnation arrive

holding hands,
welcome them both.
They may open a door to that Beloved.

And when that door finally opens,
you will find
neither denial nor damnation
on the other side.

Attar urges us to wake from slumber and begin our Wayfaring journey. Take the first step, he says, and the second will inevitably follow. Movement is key. Yet, he also warns, beware, your journey toward the Divine is never constant. There are dark nights of the soul when you don't feel the Beloved's presence, but also times of elated bliss when you find luminous grace in the most unexpected places.

When you enter the Ocean of Wisdom
a wave may swell and push you back,
another may embrace and fling you forward.

That's how it is with the Almighty.

Sometimes you're chased from the temple door.
Other times mysteries unveil to you in a heathen den.

We slow down our journey when we run after money and fame without any regard for others. We fret over how we are viewed on social media: if we are thin enough, pretty enough, tall enough, muscular enough, religious enough, or smart enough. Instead of seeing ourselves through the eyes of the only true Friend, we busy ourselves with believing the lies of the material world.

If the Almighty is a stranger on the outside,
don't worry,
on the inside, that Beauty is the Friend.

We stray from the Path when we busy ourselves with judging others and dictating how they should or should not live, worship, or behave.

Don't puff yourself up so pompously
or you'll stray from the Path in disgrace.
There is no room here for pride,
or self-importance,
or the things you value and hoard.

He warns that such fruitless pursuits trap us in our own puddles of fancy. Some souls spend a lifetime splashing in it and eventually drying up in the puddle they mistake for the sea.

When you find your joy in a puddle,
the water around you will ignite
into a circle of fire.

Don't fall into a deep wet slumber.
Each drop of that water
washes away your honor.

When a soul is mindful of and persistent in its own Wayfaring journey, it ultimately advances far enough to achieve the state of *fana*—the disappearance of the self from the ego-self, meaning one's lesser self, that upholder of self-righteousness and self-proclaimed truths.

You minus your ego-self
equals
your true essence.

To help clarify this idea, let's think of it metaphorically. Imagine you are a drop of water that after a long journey has finally arrived at the shore of an ocean. You join that great body of water and in doing so you cease to be yourself. You become your potential: the ocean. In other words, you recover your true self. In the same way, when you achieve this state of oneness with your Creator, religion or faithlessness, virtue or vice, will all disappear and become utterly irrelevant. Attar likens us to a mirror reflecting the sun. You can say I am the sun and that is true enough, yet you are also a mirror. The less polluted that mirror is with dirt and dust, the better it can reflect the attributes of the sun. You would be a bearer of its light, but the sun is the possessor of its attributes in perfection.

Polish the mirror of your heart,
wipe away all traces of your ego-self.

Let it reflect the light of the Divine.

The Beloved, the Almighty, the Divine, or the Creator in these poems can arguably stand for God, Allah, the Universe, Jehovah, Dios, Jah, or any other Supreme Being by any other name worshipped in various belief systems of the world. These words ultimately point to a single Supreme Being or a state of existence beyond this physical realm. They are proxies for an entity or an idea that runs deeper than language. Attar does not side with any one faith, religion, or belief system. His aim is to guide us onto the Path and initiate us as Wayfarers.

We each travel our own path.
No two souls journey the same.

I love that Attar refuses to pander to our egos or sugarcoat the wisdom he offers. He points directly at our delusions, misconceptions, and overinflated self-regard so we can begin our Wayfaring journey immediately and without self-deception. He repeatedly warns against the soul's greatest enemy, the ego-self, which he calls "that cyclone of calamities."

If the Almighty embraces you,
you'll catch fire with joy.

This is how it works,
not in the topsy-turvy way you imagine.

Narcissists don't get this.

Attar's wisdom has changed my own life. He has lifted me from the prison yard of the world to a place I never imagined possible. Whether you devour this book from cover to cover or open it at random for guidance or inspiration, Attar's words will speak to you in the language of the soul.

If you come sad and frozen to this book,
its invisible fire will flare and melt your ice.
They are like a mystery under a veil
that reveals its beauty slowly.

Kill your fear. Step forward.
Leave faith and blasphemy behind.
Don't worry. Don't be naive. Don't hesitate.
Take the first step.

WHO IS ATTAR?

Attar (CE 1145–1220) was born in Nishapur, a city in the northeast region of Iran. "Attar" means perfume maker, which at the time also referred to interpreter of illnesses and dispenser of remedies. In today's lingo, he was a pharmacist.

He earned a living as a healer so that he would never have to seek a position in the royal court as a poet, as they were traditionally obliged to flatter their patrons.

I thank the Almighty I'm not a courtier,
free from such a degrading profession.

I haven't tasted a single bite from a tyrant's table,
nor do I have a patron for my books.

The circumstances of his death are the subject of much speculation. Some believe he died a violent death in the massacre Genghis Khan and the Mongol army inflicted on the city of Nishapur in 1221 CE. However, there are stories about the circumstances of his death that are perhaps more lore than fact. In one such story, when the Mongol invaders are outside the city gate, Attar grabs his sword and rides out to meet them in battle. When his head is cut off, he simply picks it up and continues fighting. In another version, Attar is taken prisoner by a Mongol soldier. A man comes along and offers a silver coin for Attar's release, but Attar advises his captor against selling him so cheap. The soldier's eyes glint with greed, and he refuses the sale. Soon, another buyer offers a gold coin. Again, Attar advises his abductor not to sell. The soldier refuses that sale as well. Finally, a man with a donkey sees Attar in chains and offers the soldier a sack of straw in exchange for the elderly poet's life. Attar then says: "Now you have been offered what I am truly worth." Upon hearing this, the angry soldier picks up his sword and beheads Attar with one swoosh.

Attar's philosophy and poems have influenced many great philosophers, mystics, and poets, including Rumi. Forty books bear Attar's name but only seven are verifiably his. The poems in this book are drawn from his verified books.

Today, Attar's mausoleum stands in Shadiakh, one of the main palaces of old Nishapur in Iran. He is revered as one of the great Sufi mystic masters of all time.

The Invisible Sun

Free yourself of all preachers.
Animate your heart with your Creator.

There is an invisible sun
hiding inside us all.

One day the veil falls away
and that revealed sun shines,

and in its radiant light
all virtues and corruption vanish.

ATTAR

Why do you search for the Creator's address?
There is no map, no direction.

Discard your ego-self. Begin the journey.

So long as any part of you remains,
even a strand of hair will block you like a mountain.

Creator,

If I worship you for fear of Hell,
burn me in that same Inferno.

If I worship you in hope of Heaven,
ban my soul from Paradise.

But if I worship you for You,
lead me into your Eternal Presence.

ATTAR

By the time you fill your eyes with the world,
your life has come and gone
and still you have done nothing.

Don't pander to your ego.
Don't drag your precious soul
through feces and filth.

The key
to unlock both worlds
is love.

ATTAR

Everything, large and small, honors your existence.
Don't look at yourself with contempt.
There is nothing greater than you.

The seven heavens revolve for you.
The angels pray for your sake.
Heaven and Hell are of your own making.
It is to you that the celestial spirits bow.

Eternity's clouds rain mercy to multiply your delight.
When the time comes to elevate the whole,
all robes of honor will be for you.

The Creator will forever bless you
with all the reverence and prayers of angels.

If your head is tipsy
and your heart aflame,

if you are drunk and senseless
with the wine of longing,

how could you be satisfied
with just one sip of anything?

Find the source where wine
flows and never runs out.

ATTAR

Disappear.

This ruin is not your home.
What's important is the essence.

What does it matter if truth branches or not?

When the Eternal Sun shines,
does it matter if here is an atom
or here its shadow?

When you are one with the Beloved,
you will not be the Beloved,
but be immersed in the Beloved.

There is a difference between
shifting into and being absorbed.

This is not small talk.
This is profound if you embrace it.

Once you see whose shadow you are,
you will be freed in death and life.

ATTAR

Let defeats and disappointments
fuel your power.
That's when your confused heart
sparks to life.

Let pain become your cure.

Close one eye to doubt
open the other to the Beloved's face.

Detach from the world
for nothing endures
and no one is faithful.

Loyalty is not a treasure
you can snatch
from this dragon's mouth.

ATTAR

One day you wake up and you are seventy,
and have slept your life away.

It's no use; you've made your choice.
You cannot make up for lost time,
even if you cry with a hundred thousand eyes.

There is no cure for death
but the death of desire.

Shed your worldly trimmings
like autumn leaves.

We were all born to die.
The heart is pledged to it.
The soul won't linger.

ATTAR

If you are not caught in the web of love,
you're not worth a single breath.

If your heart has not unglued its eyes,
it does not deserve to see.

If you're not a seeker in this desert,
you are pitiful as dust.

If you don't have a clue,
you're just killing time before a stone wall.

Show me the way to church,
mosque, temple, or tavern.

Wait, never mind.
They're all forbidden to me.

I'm not allowed in any house of worship,
nor do they let me into the tavern
to get myself good and drunk.

Can you ever truly tell who is a pretender,
who a Wayfarer?

Listen friend, there is another road
that meanders between them all.
Go seek it.

ATTAR

If you do not see the Beloved's face,
get up! What are you waiting for?

Go look for it!
Shame on you if you don't know the taste of desire.
Don't drift aimlessly like an idle leaf.

Don't become a slave to appearances,
or head to toe you'll be mired in mud.

Love of insight and soul-knowledge
is not feral lust-play.

Beauty wilts.
That sort of love unravels us.

ATTAR

The firestorm of separation from the Beloved
makes Hell's inferno look like a bonfire.

Whoever gives you a hundred sweet promises
is pointing you toward fire.

What is that fire? The world.
Give it up.

There is an inferno ahead.

The long road is treacherous,
the body weak,
the heart captive,
and the soul timid.

Like a lion,
warily avoid the flame.

Only the free and pure
can begin the Journey.

What more can I say?
Stop dodging the issue.

ATTAR

Have you lost your way,
seeker of secrets?

Go search for your soul's mysteries
before your life expires.

If you fail to find yourself
while you're alive,
how can you know your soul
after death?

If you keep looking for flaws,
how will you be able to see the Unseen?

Free yourself from the defects of this world.
Rejoice in the love of the Absolute Invisible.

ATTAR

Keep vigil at night.
Fast during the day.
Do it until yearning for knowledge
surfaces in you.

Yearn and seek until everything,
even the yearning itself,
evaporates.

Squash your fears,
even of savage dragons,
to fathom the Almighty.

If denial and damnation arrive
holding hands,
welcome them both.
They may open a door to that Beloved.

And when that door finally opens,
you will find
neither denial nor damnation
on the other side.

ATTAR

Lounging in a palace would be peachy
if death's hand didn't turn the world's wheel.

If you seek knowledge,
don't look with your eyes.
Don't say "I know!"

If you do,
that belief becomes your prison.

Leave this arena a wanderer.
Keep eternity in your pocket.

ATTAR

Be generous as the bountiful sea.

Be bighearted like the magnanimous sun.

Be modest as the humble earth.

If you learn love
in the realm of the mind,

you'll never know love
in the territory of the soul.

ATTAR

So long as you exist,
so does good and evil.
Lose yourself
and they too will vanish.

If you choose to dwell
in your own self,
then the good and evil
will stay with you

and the road will stretch out far
and farther.

If you're not a seeker,
you might as well be a corpse,
a lifeless shadow on a wall,
a soulless puppet or a beast.

ATTAR

Open your heart's eyes
and fuse with the universe.

If you open only the mind's eyes,
you will never see love in full.

Wayfarer, if you suffer
downfalls,
know that each fall
is a windfall.

The way to the Beloved has ups
and downs.
What can you do?
That's the way it is.

ATTAR

There is an imperishable and eternal Beauty.
It's heresy *not* to go after it.

You take a face made up of bile, phlegm, and blood
and compare it to the full moon?

If you hunt the form, you chase imperfection;
skin-deep glamour will cease and pass.

Seek what's behind the veil.
There, you will find true beauty.

Love of the Beloved must be sought from the Beloved.
It's not something one can hand out.

ATTAR

Do not give up praying, not for one instant,
yet,
when you do pray, don't worship your praying.

To seek love, forget belief, forget unbelief.
There is no place in love for faith or doubt.

A lover who steps onto the Wayfaring Path
is like a shadow cast on earth.

What shadow can remain on a road
where the sun waits in ambush?

ATTAR

So long as you are something
how can you enter nothing?

It's foolish to think anything lasts.
Wake up.
Rush toward nonbeing.

Don't get caught up in what was
in the beginning or in the end.

In the end, all that is useless.

Whatever keeps you from the Path
is an idol
that will convert you to worshipping
idols.

If there is an "I,"
there is no unity.

Toss it out
and unity is possible.

Lose yourself in the Beloved
—that is unity.

Lose even the losing
—that is oneness.

When you tie your soul's robe
with the belt of spirituality,
then you can untie
the belt of the universe.

Come, unfasten it,
open the robe and stare
at its mysteries.

ATTAR

The Beloved is a grand Ocean on which
both worlds are dancing reflections.

When the Ocean tosses and breaks,
how could patterns that shimmer
on the surface linger unbroken?

Lose yourself in this Ocean.
Find comfort in your lost state,
and your heart will calm.

When your soul is absorbed
into the Ocean, it is saved
from its own oblivion.

That's when creativity abounds
and mysteries begin to unveil.

Abandoning your self
is annihilation.

When even awareness
of annihilation
is annihilated,

you'll find eternal life.

ATTAR

The soul and the body
are intimates.

At the hour of separation
the reflection leaves the mirror.

Life doesn't pause.
It is a breath. It passes by,
so go ahead and pass by it too.

All pain and loss in this world
vanishes in a flash. Leave it.
Don't look back. Nothing stays.

Attach your heart to a single thing
and you strip it of sweet life.

ATTAR

Since all is one,
there is no two.
There is no me
apart from you.

Don't confuse unity with uniformity.
Unity can only exist in diversity.

Seek the essence;
don't be bamboozled by externals.

What's essence?
The core of everything.

What are outer forms?
Nothing.

A true Wayfarer's way is to act,
yet, we keep giving sermons.

That's the trouble.

ATTAR

Both this world and the next
are adrift within the soul.

The body hidden in the soul,
the soul secreted in the body
—each, lost inside the other.

Emerge from your confusion.
Find the core of your humanity.

Listen to truth with your heart.
Listen with your soul.
Don't listen with this body of water and clay.

ATTAR

What use is a world teeming with shadows?
What's the point of existence if nailed into one place?

A thousand mysteries had to be unveiled
to help you hurry to the base of the wall.

Wisdom of ages had to unify
to lift you to the top of that barrier.

That's when you finally woke up
from your fitful slumber.

Love is not a metaphor.
It fits into no language,
no world of words.

Love is a tongue that's spoken
in clues, hints, and signs.

Only the heart gets the essence of love.
The mind can never wrap itself around it.

ATTAR

At midnight, my silver-bodied beauty,
drunk with love, broke into my room.
I lost all my senses and blood
bubbled hot in my veins.

That enchanter offered me a cup and said:
Can you drink this and not get drunk?

I took a whiff of that wine,
and my intellect packed its bags.
Out went the light of my sanity.

I roared, leaped up,
discarded my religious robe
then tied an idolator's belt around my waist.

I became a gambler, a rabble-rouser,
highway robber and worshipper of wine.
I renounced everything "good,"
rejected all "evil," and became nothing,
everything, and nothing again.

When everything, ego, vanity, and self
were consumed,
I was finally able to let go.

If you suffer love's torment,
you're brave to the roots of your hair.

If your soul welcomes love's mysteries,
you'll happily give up everything else.

Abandon it all, stay naked.

Then what will remain is the call, "Enter!"
Then you will step inside.

ATTAR

A noble aim is a swift-winged bird,
speeding toward its goal.

It flies and sees with inner eyes.
It soars above the world, not within it.

You, whose being is mingled
with nonbeing,
you, whose joys are mingled
with grief,

take heart.

Without ups and downs,
would you ever know the meaning
of relief?

ATTAR

First, you strike bold like lightning,
but then cover yourself with rubbish
to protect against the shock.

What are you doing?

Rise up. Be a true seeker.
Don't stay in your head.

Set fire to reason, and flare
into a mad lover.

Offer your heart to the Beloved.
That invitation has no expiration date.

Turn your ego into ash.
Take the first step.

That's when you'll grasp
the architecture of love's light,

how it emanates and expands
only from the center of fire.

ATTAR

Polish the mirror of your heart,
wipe away all traces of your ego-self.

Let it reflect the light of the Divine.

You can never be the Sublime in full
but you are immortal
when you reflect the Great One.

You found true friendship
but lost it because of neglect.
Don't wait, fling yourself into full love.

Brave the dragon, your ego,
whose hunting ground is this world.
Slay that beast. That's the price of true love.

Love infuses the human soul,
transforms dragons into ants.

ATTAR

If you've had enough of this one life
then step through your soul's door
into a thousand more.

Each time you detach from one life,
myriad others are gifted to you.

And each time you transcend those lives,
countless more await you.

Why settle for half a life?
Have a full one with your Creator.

Open your yearning eye and find the Path,
then step forward and see the Great Court.

When you reach that exalted place, its glory
will loosen the world's grasp on you.

Your every breath is a jewel.
Your every atom
guides you toward the Beloved.

Head to toe, all of you
comes from that Giver.

Love is fire, mind is smoke.
When love arrives, reason flees.

ATTAR

When you find your joy in a puddle,
the water around you will ignite
into a circle of fire.

Don't fall into a deep wet slumber.
Each drop of that water
washes away your honor.

A ray of sun penetrates a dark room.
Particles appear dancing in that shaft of light.

If you grasp your own nothingness, you can braid
those specks into a rope and climb up to the sun.

But if you insist on living in your ego-self,
what else can I say? I leave you in your mirage.

ATTAR

If the Almighty embraces you,
you'll catch fire with joy.

This is how it works,
not in the topsy-turvy way you imagine.

Narcissists don't get this.

The world may seem securely yours,
but it will vanish in a wink.

How long will you make this world
your stomping ground?

Give up your pride in titles and possessions.
Stop indulging in this shadow theater.

Your garden and mansion are prisons,
blights on your soul.

Don't brim with smug vanity.
Real estate is for grazing cows.

A lover's path is without a horizon.
Boundless.

Come, quickly.

Step into it.
Your soul is at risk.

Don't busy yourself with nothings.
Nothing will come of it.

How long do you think your life's ocean will surge?

If your inner being is tainted, even a bit,
it's the same as being foul
through and through.

When something blocks your Way,
it won't matter if it's a blade of grass
or a mountain.

The Almighty's forgiveness
has more muscle than its rage.

That Great One's door
is always open to the strays.

ATTAR

Oceans and deserts lie between the Beloved and you.
The road stretches past the horizon!

Go on this journey weeping, laughing,
and riddled with amazement.

What is a gem but a sparkling,
colored rock.

Don't turn your heart into stone
hunting its glitter and rainbows.

If you grasp what I'm saying,
you won't hunt meaningless trash.

ATTAR

If you pander to your ego and leap
into depravity's flames—

the fire of lust will char your honor,
impair your reason, weaken your body,
cloud your heart, blind, deafen, and age you.

This is how Death expands its army.

Night and day they ride behind their Dark King
and when they come for you, they will arrive
from all directions.

Fanciful desires live
in the house of the ego.

The only home for sincerity
is the heart.

ATTAR

Don't build your foundation on unstable reality
for the sake of an ephemeral hour of delight.

If your mood darkens when things go wrong,
don't worry; this too is fleeting.

The Beloved has gifted you a world,
showered you with a hundred favors!

What seems tragic is a treasure
to eyes that pierce the surface.

Both worlds are your shadow.
Heaven and Hell are ornaments that hang on you.
Your soul is a mirror. It reflects your Creator.

You won't know what waits for you
until you step into that invisible beyond.

ATTAR

When they heard accounts of loving the Beloved,
stories bloomed on every storyteller's tongue.

Each person twisted the tale his own way.
Religions and beliefs multiplied.

People followed different philosophies and faiths.
The path to the Source became hard to find.

The way to the sun is one atom at a time,
but now a war rages in every particle.

Religious extremists, why so serious?
Laugh a little.

What's all this blubbering,
the rigid judgment,
the sanctimonious obduracy?

Unglue your eyes.

Today is a day of celebration.
There is wine in your cup
and sugar on your tongue.

Drunkenness and the Beloved
are an eternal pair.

True religion is the religion of love.
Come, join this drunken feast.
Here, you will hear no lies.

ATTAR

If you ask:
What should I do?

I say:
Stop doing whatever you've been doing!

Become nothing
to be absorbed.

If you remain full
of your ego

there will be no room
for the Eternal Beauty.

The universe is in awe of how
the visible Beloved
is also invisible.

That Hidden One
is in every particle of sunlight,
in every drop of rivers, oceans, and seas.

Look at the world, see how it is made.
It is all attraction, connected through love.

There is neither monotheism
nor allegory,
neither belief
nor disbelief,
and in between them
there is nothing, too.

If you commit an error,
the door of penitence is open.

So go on and repent. This door never closes.

When you are sincere
a hundred such doors
swing open to you.

ATTAR

Those who go to Paradise expecting
the promised
ambrosia

. . . well, that's all they will get

because that's all
they know and
believe.

You lay a hundred thousand snares
to gain a nugget of gold, and when you have it,
it will be time to die. The end.

Then your heirs will get the gold and
all the misery that comes with it.

What do you imagine you can take with you,
you, who light up your heart with the love of gold?

ATTAR

Hold nothing in your hands,
and the cleansing of your heart begins.

Wipe your heart clear of its own traits,
to reflect the spirit of the Divine.

The Beloved is a grand Ocean in which
the Garden of Paradise is a tiny ball of dew.

When you have the ocean, you have the drop.
Don't settle for less, don't seek anything but the ocean.

If you can find your way to vast waters,
why rush toward a drop of dew?

If you can speak heart-to-heart with the sun,
why have a conversation with a dust mote?

If you can contain the whole,
why trouble with the parts?

If you can be a soul,
why bother with limbs?

If you want to be complete, look for the whole.
Desire all, be all, become all.

Choose everything.
Choose everything.

ATTAR

When you steer beyond
presence, absence,
being, not being,
you'll finally pilot your soul.

You, minus your ego-self,
equals
your true essence.

ATTAR

Part ego and completely a heart,
you are neither one.
They are both a part of you.

Your origin is in neither one.
Don't indulge in either.

If you do, you'll never find
your essence.

Conniving, suspicious, unkind heart,
catalog your own vices.
Keep tabs on your own failings.
Look at your own flaws. Don't be blind.

Maybe then, you'll have less time to nitpick others.

Whatever sin you have committed
there is none greater
than humiliating and insulting
a fellow human being.

One day you look in the mirror and find
you've aged in less than the wink of an eye.
"Seventy!" you marvel.

But that is not the surprising part.
What's astonishing is that your ego
glows brighter than ever.

You may say: "I was deceived by the world,"
and yet look how you continue to wrap
your proud heart in silver and gold.

When life overflows with wealth,
your share of wisdom drains away.

You want to live longer so you can
gather more wealth? Go ahead, do it,
but beware
that at the hour of your soul's departure
all you've hoarded will pile
heavy on your back.

ATTAR

What you call "happiness" in this world
does not even resemble true joy.

Here, where the ego is a blazing fire,
show me a single sunny heart.

If you swivel like a compass around the world,
you won't find a heart that is truly content.

You can join with the Beloved.
That's the gift concealed within you.

Those who say: *I've cracked that mystery*,
are insane idiots.

Adam was like a bird who sought that seed
but instead flew into a snare.

If you are deep asleep,
what can I say? Slumber well.

The one who joins with the Beloved
has learned how to disappear.

ATTAR

Beloved, if loving you makes me an infidel,
then so be it.
Let that be my religion.

When souls first step onto the Wayfaring Path
they boast with certainty and conviction.

But all that is only fantasy and fancy delusions.

What does a drop of polluted water
know about the sea?

When a veteran drinker gets drunk,
he runs around and says:
"The world is under my command."
But when he at last sobers up,
he shrinks from shame for even thinking that.

If you say you are drunk with love,
know that even *that* is a deception.

The only way to see the face of the Beloved
is to set fire to your vain imaginings and ego.
The only ticket to the Almighty's court
is nothingness.

For lovers of the Almighty,
there is no war, no peace.

Lovers don't gauge distances
in kilometers or miles.

If you don't get this,
what are you doing here?

The heart's bird
is from an uncharted nest.
It does not chirp
the language of the mind.

ATTAR

The world is a wildfire that eats all creatures.

Be a fearless tiger.
Escape the fire.
Don't burn like a moth,
crisping in your own delusion.

If you hesitate in the act of love,
how can you bare its mysteries?

If you want to touch love's secrets,
strip off your armor, embrace its pain.

ATTAR

Seek your path in the valley of love.
Lose yourself to find the way.

When you walk the path to the Beloved,
you will find the precious gem concealed
in the folds of your soul.

Each adornment you hang on yourself,
will one day burst into ash.

When you drown in the material world,
your faith drowns too.

Spill your wealth in all four directions.

What makes you think you can hold on
to money, property, this or that,
when even your life is not yours to keep?

Better to be infamous in love
than famous for crown and riches.

So many on this earth are charlatans,
impostors chasing the world and its carrion.

Love has no address.
If you want to find it
then forget self and walk deep
into nothingness.

Let go of this desert world,
discover the treasures folded
into your soul. That's how
you travel a lifelong journey in a flash.

Wake up, your life is passing by.
Don't delay, the caravan is leaving.

ATTAR

When your soul rises
from itself
without its self,
it will finally be alone
with the Beloved.

Knowledge is the everlasting realm.
Seek it. Achieve it.
But stay content with this world,
and you'll be forever lost.

Get drunk with soul-knowledge
and the nine skies will become
a skiff on your sea.

You'll soar above everyone
and the earthly dominions will seem
small as a single seed.

If the world's sovereigns could taste
a draught from that boundless Ocean,
they'd keen in grief and avoid
each other's eyes from stinging pain.

ATTAR

Lately, my soul lingers
on the tip of a hair,
and that hair belongs to You.

Each curl, every wave,
leads to a temple,
and inside that temple
lives only love.

To reach the Beloved,
forget your own self.

There is no other way.

Fanciful veils of illusions
hang between you and your Creator.

The ego is the thickest of them all.

ATTAR

You see all this, hear it all and yet
fail to turn away from your ego.

Your journey has become long and grueling;
how long will you listen to ignoramuses?

Not until you die to your ego and to the world
will your soul break free from your throat.

Turn your back to this sphere of dust
or else you are truly dead.

Don't miss the mysteries behind the veil.

Do you love the spectacle of drums and flags?
Then you are not a Wayfarer but a dead thing.

That hollow sound you hear is just the wind
that flaps the flag and beats the drum,
a clamor worth less than the half note of a single beat.

If your heart grasps the pain of love,
it can fathom it too.

But if you declare:
"Look how I love!"
that deliberate awareness
becomes a barrier
between you and your love.

What kind of a drunk is aware
of their own drunkenness?

If you want your soul
to advance in love,
then love
without obsessing over
the act of love.

Have mercy on the merciless,
the Great Merciful will bless you.

Point a finger at a so-called sinner
and you become an avenging tyrant.

The Beloved has access to all hearts,
but a wayward heart can't know that Presence.

If the Almighty is a stranger on the outside,
don't worry,
on the inside, that Beauty is the Friend.

Don't spend your dear sweet life
counting your losses and gains.
What is "profit" when you pay
for everything with your soul?

ATTAR

This material world is a rickety bridge
that connects you to the other side.
Every second a part of it crumbles.

Child, this isn't a place to lounge around.

What heart is harmed
when given to the Beloved?

Give yours.
That Friend cherishes your heart.

Death cannot darken
what's been lit up.

ATTAR

Don't puff yourself up so pompously
or you'll stray from the Path in disgrace.
There is no room here for pride,
or self-importance,
or the things you value and hoard.

Each night angels descend
from the Almighty's highest peak
for your sake,
and yet
you don't stir in your bed.

A welcoming cohort comes for you
from that pinnacle,
but you make yourself scarce.

Pity that you don't get it—
this honor offered to you.

ATTAR

If your love is really true,
your beloved will at last
become your true lover too.

An iota of love
is better than all the worlds.

A morsel of lovers' pain
is better than the lovers themselves.

Love is the magnetic core
that draws everything together,
but beware:
There is no perfect love without pain.

ATTAR

No one can see the Beloved's face,
so that Giver has given us a mirror
to gaze at its reflection.

That mirror is the heart.
Look for the Beloved there.

When the eye focuses on the sun,
dust motes shimmer, blur, and disappear.

ATTAR

In the dust storm of nothingness
you face annihilation, certain doom—
yet march on like a clueless ant.

The cosmos pulls you along bit by bit.
You pass your days pleasantly enough
and neglect your soul.

Wake up, friend!

Stay watchful
in the alleys of the heart,
where thieves lie in ambush.

Keep your heart jewel
safe from their gaze.

On the Wayfaring Path
knowledge splits
into unnumbered insights.

One person finds it
in a church or a mosque,
another in a shrine for idols.

Was, is, and will be
are like three floating particles.

Don't focus on them.

Instead, ask yourself:
What source illuminates them all?

You were fashioned by your Creator
and bowed to by angels.
You are that spectacular!

You are so loved that the world
reels and spins around you.

Don't be blind to who you truly are:
you, who exist in both worlds,
you, who wear the sky's blue dome
like a turquoise ring on your finger.

When you enter the Ocean of Wisdom
a wave may swell and push you back,
another may embrace and fling you forward.

That's how it is with the Almighty.

Sometimes you're chased from the temple door.
Other times mysteries unveil to you in a heathen den.

ATTAR

If you arrive at the Beloved's Ocean
a polluted soul, it will not refuse you,
you will merely sink to its floor
and remain yourself.

But if you come as a pure
drop of water, you will lose
yourself in its vast expanse.

The Ocean's currents
will become yours,
its radiant beauty yours, too.

You will be and not be.
How can that be?

It's beyond mind's comprehension.

Expect and don't expect.
Abandon greed for work,
yet keep on task.

Don't obsess over *how* you are doing.
Instead, look at *what* you do.

Don't value what you do but
increase your doing of it.

Abandon work yet work with abandon.
Work little but work hard at working.

Be independent and be detached,
whether you're a musician
or a professional mourner.

ATTAR

We each travel our own path.
No two souls journey the same.

A fly can flap its wings all it wants,
but how can it keep up with the wind?

Wake your soul up
and you'll see that both
a manly beard and silky womanly locks
are useless except as napkins.

If you regard yourself longer
than a half blink of an eye,
you will become your own idol.

In the end what do you imagine
remains of you
but a handful of bones and rotten marrow?

Don't you know life is the wink of an eye,
that you're born to die and ride the wind as dust?

Each twilight the sun travels sword in hand
chopping off heads and filling the sky's
inverted bowl with blood.

Whether you are a sinner or a saint,
you're just a drop of water mixed with dust.
Have you ever seen a drop of water battle the sea?

When the end comes, even if you were
the monarch of the world,
nothing you could say or do would save you
from rejoining the earth.

ATTAR

If you're not guttering out
like a candle,
don't go around bragging
about your sacrifices.

The moment you boast of risking
everything for the Path,
you've contradicted yourself
in that same sentence.

Wayfarer, if you swallow
a breadcrumb in greed,
in that same instant
you've smacked yourself in the neck.

When the invisible gifts you sight
you see the heart of love.

ATTAR

You are standing at the foot
of an invisible wall,
and what you see is nothing
but your own shadow.

Smash the wall,
step through.

Both worlds are treasures in your pocket.

Look for the fire that blazes
at the core of your being.
Don't be distracted by the smoke
that shimmies around it.

Focus on that glowing flame,
and your eyes will blink away
everything superficial
and will see beyond illusions.

Pay attention!

If you let your eyes look away
from that fire at your core,
the encircling smoke will blind you.

ATTAR

This world gives you no name, no home.
Give it up when you've seen enough.

Look closer.
It is just a dreary void.

If your motivation is noble,
whatever you seek will present itself.

Even a particle of such ardor
can ensnare the sun inside an atom.

ATTAR

You are angel and devil woven together.
Sometimes you seek the angel,
other times, worship the devil.

You imagine you are alive,
but you are lounging snug and comfy
in your grave.

What are you doing?
Break away from the core of your ego.

Occupy yourself with the essence
of the Beloved.

Do you want to come to the Beloved's house?
Then come alone. Bring no other.

Rid yourself of your *self.*
Wear the garment of nonbeing.

Put on the headdress of wisdom and faith.
Thrust your head into your chest in humility.

Put your feet in the stirrups of nonbeing,
and gallop that steed toward the void.

Around your nothing waist,
wrap the belt of annihilation.

Erase your eyes, then open them.
Line them with the charcoal of nullity.

Lose yourself, then lose losing yourself,
and still lose yourself some more.

Do it calmly, again and again until
you reach complete oblivion.

ATTAR

Don't ever utter "I,"
for in that word catastrophes lie.

Shatter your arrogance.
Burn your pride.

If you stay steeped
in self-conceit and self-delusion,
you'll never know truth.

Annihilate your ego
and even if you are a dark night
passing through yet a darker night,
you will be born into light.

If you don't feel the ache of yearning,
pour the road's dirt upon your head.

ATTAR

A true lover is one with fire.

A true lover ignites,
flames and flares afire.

Give up your eyes so that you may see.
If you are told to abandon your faith
or commanded to give up your self,
who are you to refuse?

Renounce them both.

Naysayers say this is blasphemy.
Tell them: Love is above heresy and faith.

What does love have to do with belief or unbelief?
What do lovers have to do with life's trappings?

Love insists on the heart's pounding pain.
Love demands a gnarled and arduous tale.

ATTAR

The mind can't master the art of love.
Love cannot engage in the brain.

True love comes with a passion
that sometimes shreds the veil,
other times mends it.

ATTAR

So long as you cling
to the idea of Heaven and Hell,
your soul will not know
the Divine mystery.

Free yourself
from these notions
and dawn upon dawn
will break your night.

If you are attached
to even a single particle
of the physical existence,

you'll remain
a prostrating submissive,
slave to its charm.

Mad with love for the Beloved
how could you care about your own existence?

When a fish finds the ocean,
it gives up land.

A piece of dry bread that falls into the sea
yields itself and absorbs the water.

If you are swayed by love,
virtues will blossom
where you once saw only vices.
How could One with such compassion
ever ignite with fury over an offense?

Grudge has no place in the Beloved's Ocean.
There, all sins dissolve like clouds into tears.

ATTAR

Your body is part; your soul is the whole.
Do not debase body or soul.

First, your soul was created,
then your body.
When your soul received breath,
your limbs became manifest.

Body is not separate from the soul,
it's a part of it.
Soul is not separate from the universe,
it's a part of it.

Since numbers and fractions
have no meaning on the eternal Road,
how can there be any talk of a whole or parts?

Looking for a lucrative trade?
Buy love and sell your ego-self.
A moment without love
is a loss you will never recoup.

So, what are you waiting for?
Awaken your heart, lift it
from the grave of your ego.
There is nothing more rewarding.

Bathe your body with the blood of perception.
There is nothing more sacred.

ATTAR

If all you do is give lip service about love,
then empty love-talk is all you deserve.

Love's secret is at the core of the soul.
The hangover pain you sometimes feel
is from peeking through the cloak of its mystery.

Make gold your mate, and you'll scare
even the Devil.

For a mere morsel
you'll be stingy, a sly cheat.

Your arms will be weighed down,
yet you'll be a person of no weight.

When it comes to belief and faith,
you'll drag your foot like a limping ass.

You'll become a magnate of cheating,
an illiterate in faith.

Waylaid and robbed by gold,
you'll tumble and drown in its well.

ATTAR

When someone praises you falsely,
your ego brightens with that lie.

Don't worry that life is hard, and you'll find it.

One night in your drunken love and sorrow,
the path suddenly becomes manifest.

You spring to life and taste the eternal water,
rediscover the sun hidden beneath the Beloved's hair.

One look and you lose beliefs and unbeliefs,
become a mystic and find new faith.

Inside this kind of pain, you discover the cure.

ATTAR

When a door is cracked open,
sunlight pours in.
Shadows suddenly vanish.

What remains will be the Sun and you.

Claim to be a leader on the Path,
and you'll become baser than dust.

But if you step onto the Path as a Wayfarer,
the crown of love materializes on your head.

Give up your ego
and fly out of prison.

When you become nothing,
good and evil become nothing too.

ATTAR

The shadow yearns to merge with the sun
but cannot.

Clearly, it is impossible.
Yet the shadow thinks of nothing else.

This folly is the absurdity of love.

Compassion is a sun that illuminates
all the atoms that float in its rays.

ATTAR

Beneath the curtain of your ego
lie sleeping snakes and scorpions.
Touch them lightly and they'll wake,
rise like a hundred dragons.

We all carry an inferno of creatures.
If you pander to your ego,
they will be your hellish company.

But if you rid yourself of snakes
and scorpions one by one,
you'll sleep sweetly inside the earth.

Don't carry them with you.
They will sting and bite to the end of time.

If you see the Beloved in everything,
you'll know nothing but the Beloved.

You will be in the Beloved,
from the Beloved,
with the Beloved,
of the Beloved,
and outside the Beloved, too.

ATTAR

When in love, don't say:
My pain is a shoreless sea.

Say:
My love is without a horizon.

True lovers know each other by their scars.

ATTAR

If you discriminate between a gem
and a pebble the Beloved has given you,

if you feel loved because it is a diamond
or demeaned because it's a common rock,
then this journey is not for your soul.

What does it matter, jewel or rock?
Look at the hands that gifted it to you.

A grief-stricken man cried:
"A friend whose face refreshed my soul
died yesterday, and now I am dying of grief.
His loss has darkened the world for me."

The sage replied:
"Give your heart to the Friend who does not die.
Then you will not have to die of grief,
confounded, sitting in sorrow's blood."

A sense of justice is better than a lifetime
of throwing yourself to the ground in prayer.

Don't sit in this jail of a world.
Rise up! Leave your junk behind!

How much of it will be of any use?

ATTAR

The shapes of everything in existence
are shadows of the Creator.

If that Beloved unveils its face to you,
you will see all things in this universe
as shadows cast by that unveiling.

What shadow is ever separated from its maker?

You may ask, if I lose myself in that Glory's shadow,
then how can I attain its presence?

This is how:

When a door is cracked open,
sunlight pours in. Shadows suddenly vanish.
What remains will be the Sun and you.

Beware of those who pretend to serve the Almighty.
A hundred false gods hide under their robes.

ATTAR

Don't be like an ant caught under a bowl
going round and around that inverted hollow.

Grow wings, take flight.

Lose yourself,
let no trace of you remain.
Then you'll find your way
to the Beloved.

Should even a scrap,
slight as a single strand of hair,
remain from your ego,
it will pluck you back here.

ATTAR

There is no higher rank
than private or public service.

Don't be conceited, pontificating this and that.
Just serve.

This worthless world is nothing
but heartache, headache, and turmoil.

You swim in the puddle of fancy,
your heart making a mess.

Life rushes by in hours drained of hope
while highbrows debate the intricacies of being.

All this useless preoccupation and conjecture
will pummel you under the wheel of time.

ATTAR

If you are a seeker, behave like one.
Don't pretend you're a conqueror.

That crown you've placed
on your head

is just a dense mass
of weight.

It's nailed you down here.

If you can't find the Beloved,
that Beauty is not lost.
You just don't know where to look.

Those who spill blood in tyranny
become dusty nothings in tombs,
laid to rest beneath the earth,
restless, un-resting.

ATTAR

You are made of dust.
The world too is made of dust.
Figure it out.
Don't pile more dust upon your dust.

So you seek eternal life?

Look past the shell
into the kernel of everything.

Become blind to all things
except the Beloved.

A hundred thousand mysteries
will be unveiled to you.

No matter how far you look,
no matter how wide,
your heart's eye will never see
what lives at the core of the soul.

You do what you always do
and never worry about the angel
of death at your heels.

Life dashes faster than you think.
Don't be deaf to these words.

The cotton you've stuffed in your ears
is cut from your own shroud.

ATTAR

Don't focus on your own sighs.
A sigh has an "I" at its heart,
and narcissism twice as many.

Distracted heart, you've spent your time
in an absent mind, in useless pursuits.
Where will you find another lifetime to correct this?

ATTAR

Don't play games hiding your secrets.
The universe is a crafty whistleblower.

Your heart is restless and panics
when it must cross
the bridge over an inferno.

Don't worry.

That fire is a lamp's flame,
smoking soot,
shadowy as a crow's feather.

When will the wind of pride
depart from your mind?

Look how the wheels of the mill
keep running over your head

and how your hair has turned camphor
from all that dust.

Haven't you had enough?

The only closed doors are your own eyes.
Keep looking.
The Creator's door is always open.

ATTAR

If, like Jesus, you possess
even a single needle,
a hundred thieves will block your way.

Hang on to a single eyelash,
and the road to the Beloved
will stretch impossibly long.

Seek those who have pursued knowledge
with zeal and curiosity.

Shun those who have hunted knowledge
for glory, prizes, and fame.

ATTAR

Don't be deluded by the phantasmal
light of your ego.
It's entangled in illusions,
mired in imaginings.

Watch out!

Your ego brightening the way
is a scorpion's sting.
It is death.

Release the fantasy of being,
and true being will wrap around you.

But stick to the illusion of fact,
and from its nothing you will gain more nothing.

ATTAR

The path is long, and your eyes look
but cannot even see the pits in the road.

If all your life you seek solitude,
how can you progress
without a guide on the Path?

You must walk with a wise one.
Do not walk the Path alone.
Do not plunge blind into the sea.

If you are graced by such fortune,
even a thornbush in your hands
will burst into flowers.

If these pages pointed you to the Path,
stripped the veil from your eyes,
or comforted your spirit,
then be generous to this poet in your thoughts.

ATTAR

Prayers for the Dead

My Creator, my Beloved,
I'm a tiny lost ant deep in your well.
I do not know where I come from,
where I stand, what or who I am.

Bodiless, luckless, destitute,
distracted and timid,
I have spent a lifetime simmering
in the blood of anguish.

Life has not yielded any profit to me,
and for all that I've committed,
a penalty has been exacted.

Death rests on my lips.
My life has wound down.
My heart has eluded me.
My faith has strayed.
My form is disappearing.
All meaning has evaporated.

I am caught in the crack of your door,
but my lips are still on the wall of fantasy.

Open the door wider for helpless me.
Show the Way to this lost one.

When I lie beneath the earth, Beloved,
and all hopes of exit are crushed,
when that last shovelful of dirt hits my face,

do not turn your countenance away from me.
Forgive everything and forget.
Do not throw my sins at my face.

ATTAR

Beloved, my Creator,
language cannot hold your mysteries.
Words cannot unfold your attributes.

I cull the secret of loving you,
but cannot roll it off my tongue.
And when I try to speak without language,
that telling falls short, too.

A tiny sliver of your essence would not fit
in all the dimensions combined.
A single grain of your love cannot be contained
in all the granaries of the world.

I long to be with you, but my roaring
boundless sighs don't fit inside this mouth.

I leave the Earth yearning for your love,
but it's a craving too large for this world.

What I carry back to you is a part of you,
too endless to fit inside the sky.

My religion
is to become less each day.
My faith
is to become nothing in everything.
Words are useless.
Only blood-tears can speak of how I feel.
My work in this world is done.
I travel toward the Friend's home,
riding the rotating universe.
Once you mount up, a breeze streams
and unbolts your eyes.
You pass a hundred worlds in a single breath,
and breathlessly realize:
This is only the beginning.

ATTAR

O the Originator, the Grantor of Grace,
you are the sum of all goodness.
I am a dewdrop in your Ocean.
The world of appearance cannot contain you
for you are the absolute Self-Sufficient.
Beloved, overlook and forgive my shame and grime.
Hide my foolish deeds even from my own eyes.

I come from captivity, drowned in misery.
I come in wonderment; head as lost as my legs.
I come empty-handed, a slave, dust,
a zero at your feet.
By your grace, do not reject this servant.
Clothe this wretch with garments of honor.
Purify and cleanse this stained soul.
Bury me in the ground as a faithful one.
When my body is hidden under dirt and mud,
overlook all that I have committed, good or ugly.
You created me freely, as was just.
Now forgive me freely, for that is justice too.

Honorable Bestower, be my friend
at the hour of my last breath,
for when life expires
there is no one else but you.

When my good companions relinquish
my body to the earth,
extend your hand to me, Beloved, so that I
may grasp the sleeve of your grace.

At the hour I leave this fleeting Earth,
they will ask:
What good have you done? What evil?

Without the Creator's mercy,
name, title, deeds,
or place of birth are of no use.

Not even bitter tears
shed from a thousand eyes.

Dear Restorer, please see me,
absolve and delete my errors.

ATTAR

Beloved, I have fallen.
Be the one who takes my hand.

I am chained in this prison pit,
who else but you can reach
into such a deep well?

My body is sullied from this jail.
My struck heart is tired and weak.

Forgive me if I have approached your door
grimy, filthy, and soiled.
I come from the pit.

An elbow in this world and a foot in the next,
I am neither faithless nor a person of faith.
I stand bewildered between the two.
What can I do?
I am muddled and helpless.
What's to be done?

That Eternal Seer says,
"Enter, you are worthy of the Way"
to one who has harvested oceans from tears,
and "Leave, you have no business here"
to eyes that do not know blood-tears.

It's true that I have no provisions for the Road,
but I have gallons of tears and piles of sighs.

Great One, the Merciful, the Forgiver,
let my sighs burn away my sins,
let my tears flush away my grimy deeds.

Beloved, Ever-Acceptor of Repentance,
I may be abject and poor,
but I have plenty of tears and lots of sighs.
If these are legal tender in your court,
then this servant is rich in merchandise.

Let my sighs blow clean my soul.
Let my tears wash the book of my life.

I have lost my way to You,
and my heart's beacon is grimy
with the soot of my foolish deeds.

Guide me and wipe clean the chalkboard of my life
in this world and the world to come.

A Note from the Translator

Wilhelm von Humboldt, the eighteenth-century Prussian philosopher and linguist, places language in a realm he calls a "third universe." This universe of language mediates between the "empirical world" (the outer consciousness) and the internalized structures of a society. He proposes it is only in the language matrix that our experiences assume order and are absorbed and understood. Therefore, to carelessly transport poetry from one language to another without understanding its cultural matrix is akin to literary murder. In such a case, the translator delivers to the reader not a living poem, but rather its corpse—sometimes in recognizable form, other times horrifyingly battered and misshapen.

I am a bilingual, bicultural poet. I view poetry as the essence of language, and language is deeply rooted to our collective consciousness. It is fed by allusions and expressions, secrets and history. Translation is magic, but the kind that can only occur if the translator is willing and able to re-create with selfless dedication, musical sensitivity, skillful precision, and poetic sensibility. The poems transported from one language/culture to another must breathe on their own yet reflect the essence and beauty of their original selves.

I spent years studying Attar by cutting into the bone and marrow of his poems. Once I was comfortable with the music, meaning, humor, and intention of his work, I began the process of selecting, and then re-creating the poems in English. My task was to transport the power of Attar's structurally and linguistically complex poems from their twelfth-century universe to the twenty-first-century realm of English speakers without changing their inner core.

However, there are several points I wish to clarify regarding these translations/re-creations.

- Attar uses several words for "I," meaning the self that is not the soul. In this book ego stands for our lesser self, the upholder of self-righteousness and self-proclaimed truths. Do not confuse it with "identity."

- The word "death" or the expression "to die" in these poems often refers to dissolving one's ego or letting go of one's lower self.

- Gender nouns and gender pronouns are absent in Persian. I am particularly mindful of that, especially as a female writer and translator. There is no reason to assign sex to the Divine, or to spiritual entities. The human soul is free of such physical attributes.

- And finally, it is important to note that the *Prayers for the Dead* section are poems I have assembled from Attar's large body of work. I believe they are beautiful words that could either accompany other prayers or words recited at memorials.

This book is the result of years of hard work and my unbounded love for Attar. Putting this spiritual collection together in Persian and then re-creating it in English was a monumental task that would not have been possible without the support of many beloveds, scholars, and friends. Dr. Mahmoud Omidsalar and Dr. Mohsen Emadi generously answered my many questions about complex stanzas. UCI's departments of Social Sciences and Comparative Literature, as well as the Jordan Center for Persian Studies and Culture, provided me with space and support as a writer-in-residence. My agent Ana Gosh and the editorial staff at HarperCollins, particularly my editor Gabriella Page-Fort, believed in this book and helped birth it into this world in a beautiful format. Thank you, all.

During the completion of the book, my beloved seventeen-year-old niece, Shirin Conner, exited this ephemeral world. For her sake and the sake of our children, may *The Invisible Sun* illuminate whatever space it travels through.

—Sholeh Wolpé

About the Author

Attar (also known as Shaikh Farid-ud-Din and Attar of Nishapur) was born in 1145 in Nishapur, a city in the northeast region of Iran. Reliable information on Attar's life is scarce, but what we do know for certain is that he was a pharmacist, a dispenser of remedies, and an interpreter of illnesses. Indeed, the name "Attar" means herbalist and perfume maker. Although information about his life and death is opaque and has been mythologized over the intervening centuries, at some point Attar traveled widely and met with several Sufi masters. Legend has it that Rumi met Attar when he was a child. Rumi, who later became a beloved poet, repeatedly acknowledged Attar as his master, and the influence of Attar's wisdom and style of writing is evident in his work. Attar lived for more than seventy years and died a violent death in the massacre inflicted by the Mongols in 1221.

About the Translator

Sholeh Wolpé is an Iranian-born poet, playwright, and librettist. Her literary work includes seven collections of poetry, several plays, five books of translations, and three anthologies, as well as texts and librettos for choir and opera. Her performances, solo or in collaboration with musicians and artists, have been hailed by audiences as mesmerizing. She has lived in Iran, Trinidad, the United Kingdom, and presently divides her time between California and Barcelona.

About the Book

The first comprehensive English collection from one of the world's most influential mystics—Attar—the twelfth-century poet Rumi called his master.

Twelfth-century Persian poet Attar (1145–1221) was revered by Rumi and though his work is beloved around the world, he is mostly unknown to English readers. Translated in simple, elegant language by award-winning poet Sholeh Wolpé—one among generations of poets influenced by Attar's poetry—*The Invisible Sun* is a beautiful treasury of Attar's most prescient poetry, offering comfort and inspiration.

Attar was one of the most important mystic Sufi poets in the East, comparable in stature and influence to John Milton in the West. In Western thought there is a sharp separation between day-to-day human experience and the transcendence of religion and spirituality. But Sufi philosophy teaches that while the soul awaits its release from the confines of the body, it can experience the other world through mystic union achieved by an inward journey to purify the self.

The Invisible Sun widely introduces the work of Attar—the master Rumi called "the spirit" and himself "its shadow"—to English-speaking readers as never before. Profound yet exquisite in its simplicity, bringing comfort and wisdom, Attar's poetry continues to resonate today:

Everything, large and small, honors your existence,
don't look at yourself with contempt.
There is nothing greater than you.